The Dos and Don'ts of (
Growing

Written by Luke Barnes and Luke Shackleton
Illustrated by Eleanor Jones

Don't – Over-water your orchid

Do - Water your plant like it's in a tropical forest.

Most tropical orchids grow up trees so they aren't great swimmers. In the wild, a plant experiences heavy rain followed by dry periods. When it comes to watering, give your plant a good soaking so that water runs out of the bottom of the pot, and then let it dry out again before the next watering. Watering about once a week in the winter and twice a week in the summer is about right.

Don't – Under-water your orchid

Do – Make it rain

Orchids are plants and plants need water. Although an orchid can survive for a long time without water, unlike cacti, it has not evolved in deserts and it will grow better with a good soaking, then a drying between times.

Don't – Keep your plants too hot

Do - Keep your plant comfortable

Jungles are actually cooler than you may think. The abundant foliage transpires and the evaporation cools the surrounding air. Orchids such as Cymbidiums and Odontoglossums come from cooler forests on mountains.
If you are comfortable, your plant will be comfortable too. Don't go above 28°C if you can help it.

Don't – Overfeed your orchid

Do – Give it a nice balanced diet.

Orchids, like people, can have too much of a good thing and high strengths of plant food can damage orchid roots.

As they grow quite slowly, we recommend half strength feed when in growth. A plant's ability to use nutrients depends on light levels and so it can take more food in the summer than the winter.

Don't – Keep your plants too cold

Do - Keep the ice off your orchids

Orchids grow everywhere except Antarctica so don't keep your plants with your penguins.
Phalaenopsis, Paphiopedilums and Cattleyas like it warm (min 15^0C)
Cymbidiums and Odontoglossum types can go down to ($8 - 10^0C$).
You can check the natural climate for any orchid with an internet search.

Don't - Give your plant too much light

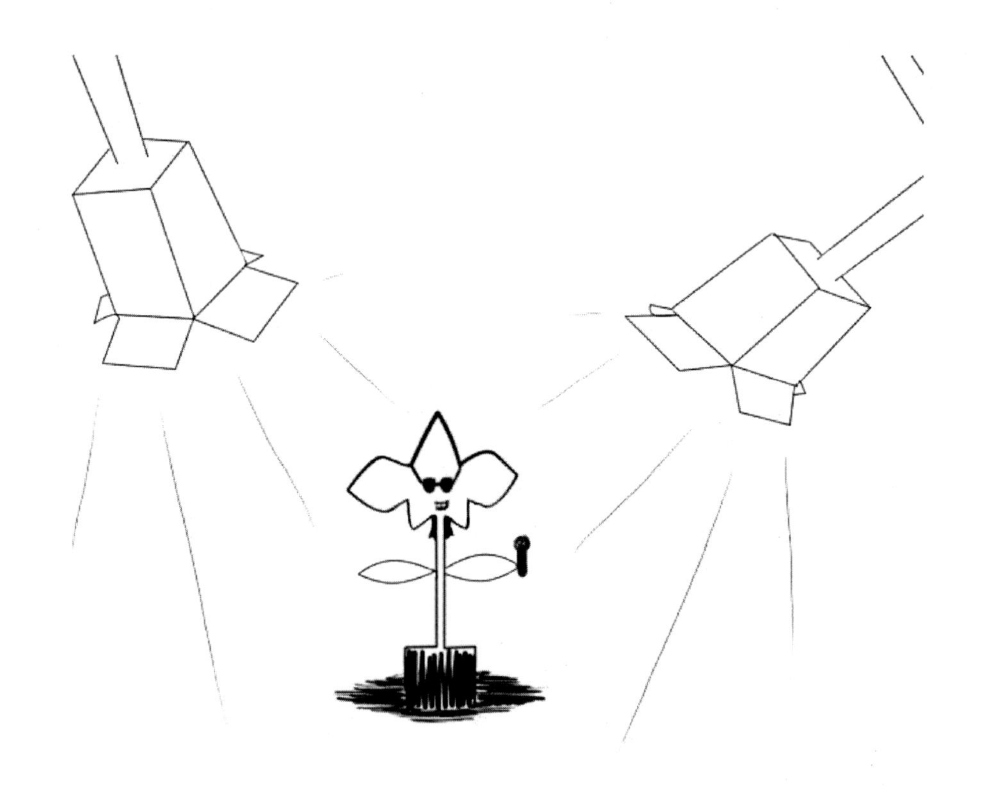

Do – Give your plant the light it needs

Sunburn is a problem for orchids, not just humans. Don't reach for the factor 50, give shade in the summer. The leaves of your plant will indicate any problems. Reddening of leaves means too much light, dark green leaves may mean too dark.

Don't - Keep your plant in the dark

Do – Give it some light

Let's face it, a cupboard is no place for a plant. Most tropical orchids grow in forest areas and live in dappled shade. In the UK, this means they need a bright spot in winter, but some protection from the Sun in summer.
Not surprisingly, some orchids naturally grow in more light than others. Paphiopedilums grow on the forest floor and need less light than other orchids.

Don't - Give your orchid too much love

Do - Give your plant some respect

If you want a cuddle, get a teddy bear. You will get to love your plants but consider their needs, not just yours.

Though some people recommend talking to your plant, we think listening is better.

Don't - Give your orchid drugs

Do – Give your plants a pure lifestyle

Don't share your vices with your plant. In fact, orchids like their water pure, rain water is excellent if you can collect it, as it has very few dissolved salts, unlike most tap water.

This means that the dissolved salts you give your plant are the ones it needs in plant food.

Don't - Grow your plant in a draft

Do - Give your orchid fresh air

Since most tropical orchids grow on trees, they get lots of fresh air in the wild.

If you grow your plants in a greenhouse or conservatory they will appreciate ventilation, but a cold draft can cause thermal shock and make the buds drop off.

Don't - Let your pet get to your orchid

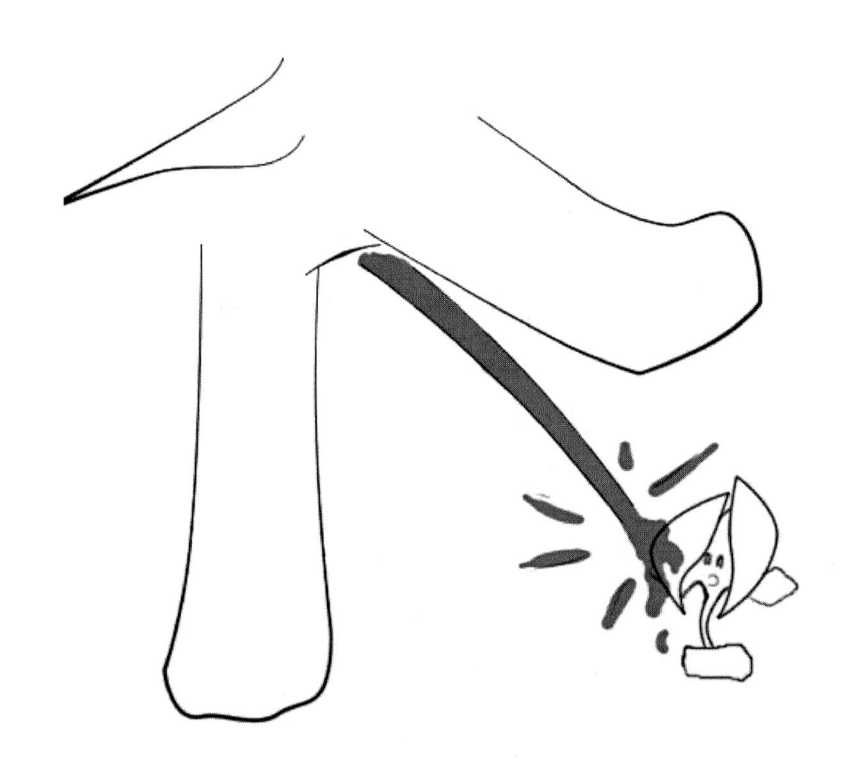

Do - Protect your orchid from attack

It may be very organic but pee is nasty acidic stuff that turns the leaves yellow. If your cat is looking guilty, check for plant poisoning.

Don't - Eat your orchid

Do- Look out for pests

Orchids taste very good to some creatures like scale insect, mealy bug and green fly. Don't let them damage or weaken your plant. Wash them off with soapy water or use a suitable insecticide. Check new plants carefully to see that you are not introducing pests to your collection.

Don't - Sit on your orchid

Do - Give your plants enough space

Orchids love their personal space. How would you like to grow all year just to be sat on? One of the biggest problems faced by any orchid grower is space. One solution may be to look for miniature orchids and that way you can fit more in. Many smaller orchids can grow well tied to a piece of cork bark, saving pot space.

Don't – Over prune your orchids

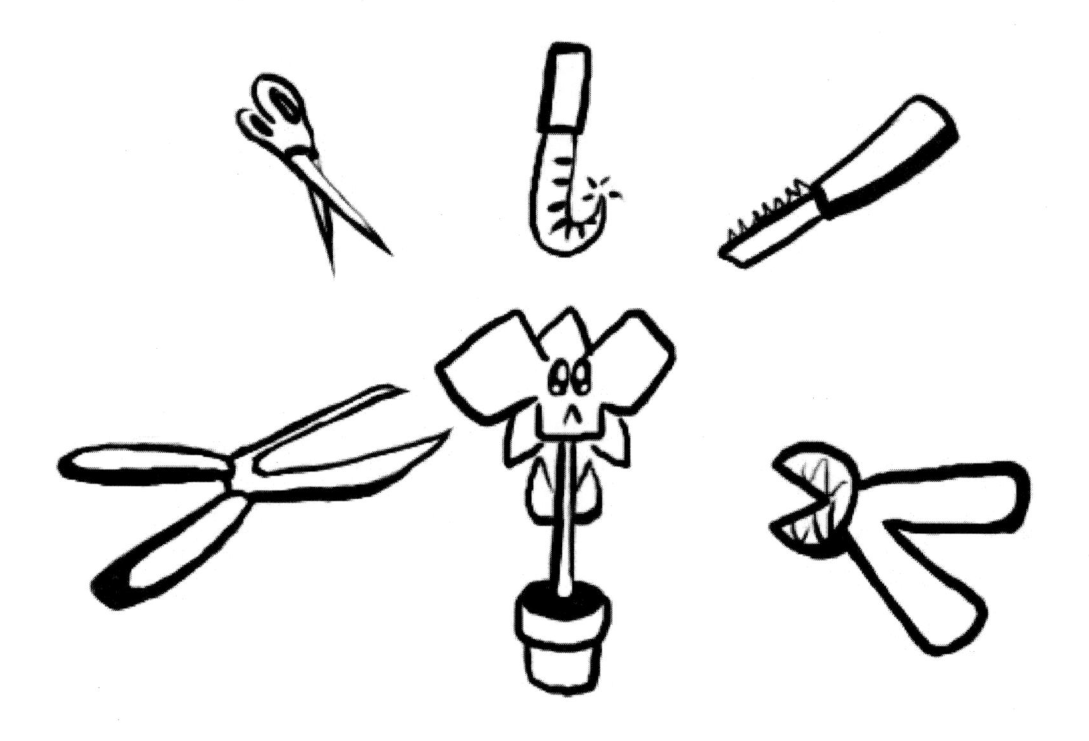

Do – Let your plants express themselves

Don't be tempted to trim aerial roots – they are supposed to be there. Old flower spikes can be removed once they are finished, remembering that Phalaenopsis can flower again from dormant buds on old flower spikes. This is also true of Psychopsis species, but Cattleya, Cymbidium, and Odontoglossums only flower once on a spike.

Don't - Use the wrong compost

Do – Give your orchid's roots the perfect environment

Orchids grow on trees, so the main component of any compost needs to be air. Bark, moss and Perlite are good, soil and peat aren't.

If you are feeling ambitious, why not try growing an orchid with no compost and tie it firmly to a piece of cork bark? You will need to spray it daily.

Don't - Over-pot your plant

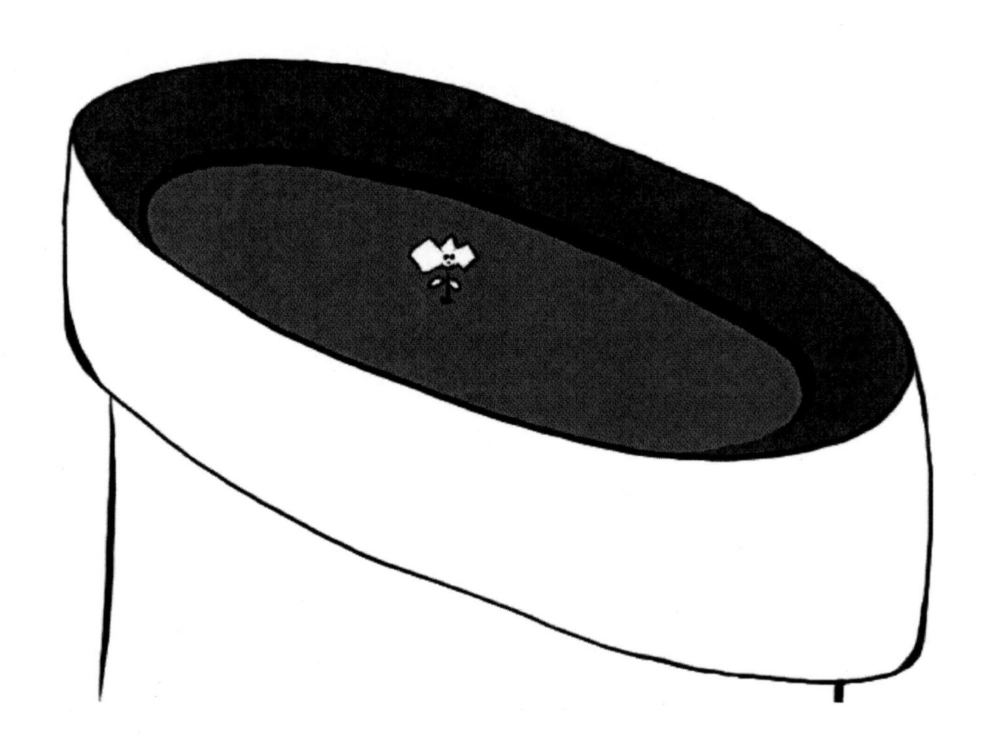

Do – Choose a pot to match your plant

It may seem weird when you buy your plant special compost to make it happy, but roots really like the gap between the pot and the compost. Using a smaller pot keeps your plant close to this magic zone.

Don't - Be impatient with your plant

Do – Show your plant some patience

The old adage applies: 'a watched plant never flowers'; they always grow when you are not looking.

One flowering a year is plenty.

Don't - Exercise your plant

Do - Let it relax

No matter how hard you train it, your orchid will never run the London Marathon.
Leaves will adapt to the light in the position it sits so don't keep moving it.

Don't - Share your fashion sense with your plant

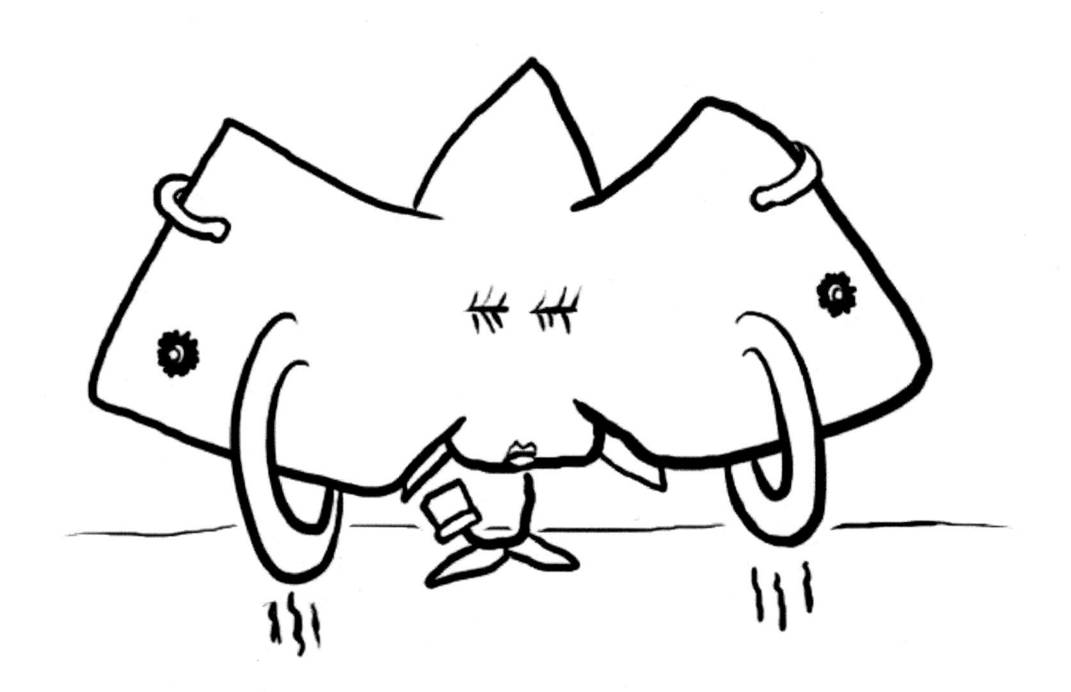

Do – Let it dress in its own unique way

Fancy clothes and sparkly jewels are great in the right place, but plants are best the way nature planned.
Get rid of any wrapping when you buy a new plant as a cocoon of polythene can trap moisture against the leaves and cause problems.

Don't - Give your plant make-up

Do - Stick to good old fashioned plant food

Be suspicious of wonder treatments that will make your plant look ten years younger or twice the size. Stick to good quality plant food.

Don't - Give your orchid books to read

Do - Let it entertain itself

It's a plant, stupid!

Even though this is called an orchid book
it is actually designed for humans to read.

Don't - Give your orchid the wrong atmosphere

Do - Give it the gases it needs

What you need is a mixture of gases containing approximately
77% nitrogen
21% oxygen
1% argon
0.04% carbon dioxide

Luckily this exists on Earth.

Don't - Treat your orchid roughly

Do - Handle with care

Orchids are amazingly tough. They will repair damage to roots after re-potting. Leave them on the dry side for about five days.

Nevertheless, keep the chainsaw locked away.

The end